# Contents

# Introduction

What can be more magical on a greetings card than some sparkle and glitter and little twinkling areas of colour? Just gorgeous, I love it.

There are some wonderful products available now which enable us to add this enchanting quality to our cards: glittery glues, amazing holographic papers, glinting jewels and lovely, soft, tinsel-like threads. All of these materials have different qualities: they glimmer and glisten, they are bright and shiny, they glow or flash or shimmer. What could be nicer? And in the spirit of the recycling philosophy which now abounds (and which we card makers have been aware of for years), many of the cards in this book have utilised any glittery things which would otherwise have been discarded – used Christmas cards, gift wrap, Christmas crackers, carrier bags, chocolate wrapping and anything I could gather without looking too conspicuously odd! My family are now used to a kind of hovering behaviour; a surreptitious glance at their wastepaper baskets; questioning looks which mean 'You're not throwing that away are you?'. I have even been known to retrieve suitable items from the dustbin, while the family looked on in quiet horror. Never mind; no-one is aware that the cards they so happily receive have very interesting histories.

I hope you will be inspired to follow some of the ideas in this book and perhaps go on to develop your own. Making cards for family and friends is one of the most pleasurable occupations, and long may it remain so.

*Polly*

*Simple designs made special by bits of sparkle. Rubber stamps, old greetings cards, metallic confetti and a used carrier bag have all helped to produce this varied collection of cards.*

# Materials

## Card and papers

In addition to the wonderful textured and patterned papers which we have become accustomed to using for our handmade cards, there are now spectacular holographic papers available. These, along with brilliantly coloured foils, make the job of card creation even more exciting. They can be used as a backdrop in contrast to matt papers, or as tiny cut-outs to add glints of sparkle. They can become shimmering borders for an otherwise subdued design or surprising inserts and inlays. They really are fascinating and the printing process and inks which create these complex images are a great wonder to me.

Sparkly card can be bought, and it is also possible to make your own using tubes of glitter, fine or coarse, liberally sprinkled on to a thin layer of PVA glue.

*Some of the many stunning papers and cards which can be used to add lustre to your card designs.*

# Glittery embellishments

Although many of these items have been around for some time, especially those associated with stamping, there are now even more available – things as diverse as sparkly pipe cleaners and shiny metal confetti; soft, tinsel-like thread, glinting net and wonderful glues positively bursting with vibrantly coloured glitter. Outline stickers are a product which can fire the imagination. They can be very intricate so the card design which includes them should be relatively uncluttered. Contrasts are always good – shiny and matt, bright and subdued, complex and simple.

*All of these items can be bought at craft stores, and they prove inexpensive when you consider how little is required for each card.*

# Stamp and embossing materials

The embossing area of stamping and the vast array of beautifully intricate stamps have given a professional look to our cards and another opportunity to discover imaginative ways of designing and presenting them. The stamps, inkpads, embossing pens and powders, and heat gun are essential for the production of all of the Fairy and some of the Butterfly cards.

*Shiny embossing powders have given a new dimension to the concept of stamping.*

**Tip**
Care needs to be taken with the heat gun; the tip can get very hot indeed.

# Other items

**Cutting tools:** Ordinary sharp scissors are essential and, if you have them, cuticle scissors are very useful for cutting out circles and other curved shapes. Circle aperture cutters are an excellent way of achieving a perfectly smooth, round opening. A good quality steel-handled craft knife is best, with some spare blades – it is possible to sharpen these on an oil stone. The knife should be used in conjunction with a self-healing cutting mat and a steel ruler. The little craft punches of heart, flower and star designs are very useful for either punching out or sticking on. Fancy-edged scissors are also an important cutting tool for the card maker.

**Glues:** I have used water-based glue sticks, PVA glue and double-sided tape throughout the book. They are all useful for different jobs. You can also use clear all-purpose glue.

**Drawing and painting materials:** You will need tracing paper and a pencil to transfer the images for some of the cards. A pencil sharpener and eraser might also be useful. Watercolour paints and brushes can be used to add colour to your cards.

**Crimping machine:** This is used to give a corrugated look to stiff paper and card. I have used it for the card on page 17 to give the appearance of snow drifting in different directions.

A **palette knife** and an **old paintbrush** are useful for spreading PVA and glitter glues.

A **knitting needle** can be used for creasing cards if you are cutting your own.

*Essential equipment used for making the cards in this book.*

# Basic techniques

## Glitter glue

1. Put the initial drop of glue on to your card then lift the nozzle very slightly. Pipe your design, allowing the trail of glue to fall on to the surface.

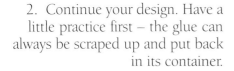

2. Continue your design. Have a little practice first – the glue can always be scraped up and put back in its container.

3. The glue can be spread on the card using an artist's palette knife to give a lovely impression of glitter dust.

# Loose glitter

1. Spread a thin film of PVA glue on to your card using an artist's palette knife.

2. Sprinkle liberally with glitter.

3. Tap the side of the card to shake off excess glitter.

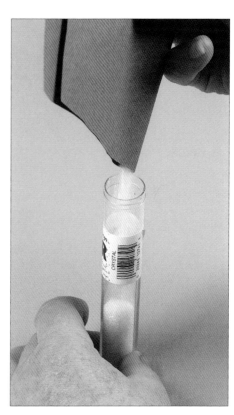

4. Pour the excess back into the container.

# Glittering Christmas Trees

This is so simple. I have used wonderful holographic self-adhesive papers for the tree decorations, all of which are cut using an ordinary office punch and small decorative punches. The indent on the planter was made with the handle of my craft knife and emphasises the rim, giving a slight 3D effect. The planter decoration was squeezed from a small glitter glue tube; this takes some time to dry so it is best to leave it until last.

**You will need**

Blank blue card,
100 x 210mm (4 x 8¼in)

White mulberry tissue,
100 x 210mm (4 x 8¼in)

Highly textured green paper,
70 x 130mm (3 x 5in)

Bright red card, 50 x 70mm
(2 x 3in)

Small piece of glittered
gold card

Various coloured
holographic papers

Red glitter glue

Office punch, little and
medium star punches

Tracing paper, pencil and ruler

Craft knife and cutting mat

Glue stick and
double-sided tape

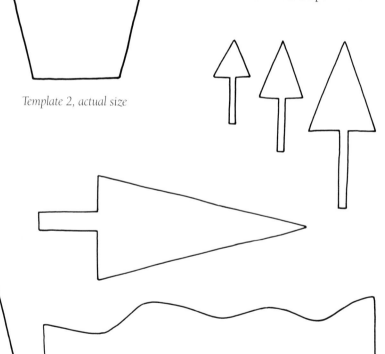

*Template 2, actual size*

*Template 1, actual size*

*Templates for the cards on pages 16 and 17, three-quarters actual size.*

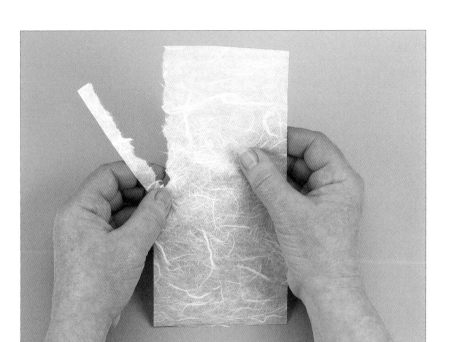

**Tip**
If making your own blank card use a thick knitting needle to score the fold (on the inside). The needle is also useful for indenting little patterns on card.

1. Tear the edges from the mulberry tissue to roughly 80 x 185mm (3¼ x 7¼in) then, using the glue stick, secure it to the card.

2. Trace the tree shape opposite (template 1) and transfer it on to the textured green paper. Cut it out and, using the double-sided tape, secure it to the mulberry tissue.

3. Attach double-sided tape to the back of the holographic papers and glittered gold card. Punch out the baubles (nine) and stars (eleven) and the gold star for the tree top. Remove the backing, using the point of your craft knife, and press the baubles and small stars on to the tree.

4. Trace the planter on to the red card and, just before cutting it out, lay your ruler along the top and make an indent with your knife handle (or a knitting needle) to create the lip edge.

6. Attach the gold star to the top of the tree.

5. Using the glitter glue, make a simple pattern just beneath the rim. When the glue has dried (a couple of hours) position the planter under the tree using double-sided tape to secure.

*Glitter glue is lovely. One is tempted to squeeze it all over the place, but a little restraint is necessary for the sake of the finished card. Here the matt, deeply textured tree contrasts well with the twinkling decorations.*

A subtly textured pearlescent paper was used as a background for this magnificent tree. I traced the tree on to a piece of dark green card, covered it with double-sided tape then cut and stuck a shimmering pipe cleaner to form the trunk. The branches were then cut and attached. The planter is matt gold card with shiny gold stars under the rim.

**Right, top:** These holographic trees were cut from a carrier bag. The central one is attached with 3D foam squares to give a slight depth to the image. The glittery snow and star (cut using a craft punch) were taken from one of last year's Christmas cards.

**Right, bottom:** For this very simple design a piece of white card was put through the crimping machine. Three sections were cut from it with the ridges going in different directions. These were attached to the blank white card using double-sided tape. The trees were cut from silver holographic paper with a self-adhesive backing.

# Shimmering Hearts

Weaving, watching something develop as you create it, is especially exciting when the paper is shimmering and shiny; seeing the piece grow as each strip is threaded through is very satisfying. Here, two contrasting papers – a crinkled foil that turns very subtly from red/gold to gold, and a small detailed holographic paper (cut from a Christmas carrier bag) – have been woven together to form a heart. This will take a little time to complete, but isn't any time spent on the one you love worth every minute? You could always gently mention 'hours of work' because your loved one will probably think you bought the card from a shop, it will look so good.

**You will need**

Blank holographic card, 135mm (5¼in) square

Matt red card, 125mm (4¾in) square

Crinkled red/gold foil paper, 105mm (4in) square

Red holographic paper, 115mm (4½in) square

Very sharp craft knife, steel ruler and cutting mat

PVA glue

*Template, actual size*

**Tip**
When cutting crinkled foil with your knife, press the ruler down very firmly and make quick jerking cuts so that the knife doesn't drag the foil and distort it.

1. Transfer the large heart on to the centre of the matt red card. Cut it out using your knife – the knife is easier to use than scissors for internal cuts.

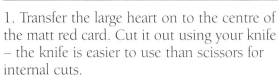

2. Using your very sharp knife, ruler and cutting mat, cut 5mm (¼in) strips in the red/gold foil, leaving a 5mm (¼in) border at the top so that the strips do not fully separate.

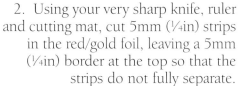

3. Repeat with the red holographic paper, but this time cut the full length of the square so that all the strips are separate.

19

4. Weave a holographic strip under and over the crinkled foil, the next one over and under, until the square is complete. Keep gently pushing the holographic strips up to keep them together.

5. Stick the woven square on to the back of the square card with the cut-out heart. Use the PVA glue, being careful not to let any squeeze out and be seen on the weaving.

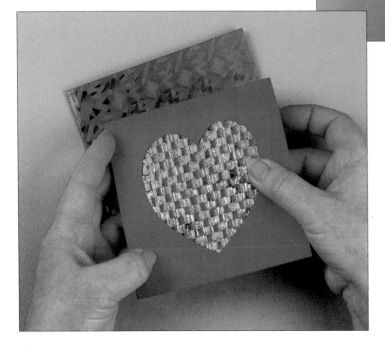

6. Run the glue along the four sides of the square and carefully position the square on the holographic card.

*This shimmering heart may take a little time to complete, but the results will be well worth the effort, and will be very much appreciated by the recipient.*

**Top:** *Delicate criss-crossing with a lovely tinsel-like thread, secured at the back of the deep pink card with sticky tape. Little Vs were cut into the edges of the card to secure the thread. The sparkling pink hearts were cut from an old Christmas card using a craft punch.*

**Bottom:** *Another simple design. Craft scissors produced the decorative edge, and the mauve sparkle for the inlay and hearts was cut from an old birthday card. The shimmering stems and dots are piped glitter glue.*

22

*This striped metallic cardstock requires a very simple design and sometimes it's nice
to disregard tradition and use colours not usually associated with the subject of hearts
and love. The five little hearts are metallic confetti secured with double-sided tape.
These are mirrored by the shiny metallic heart inlay. Silver netting adds a touch of
mystery and the little dots of glitter glue add further definition to the heart.*

# Bright Balloons

Balloons imply general partying and merriment, a subject for any celebration – birthday, anniversary, New Year, engagement; the tone can be suggested by the colours and textures. Here, the balloon is cut from striking, multicoloured holographic paper, which has the added bonus of being self-adhesive. The string is glitter glue. Have a little practice with this if you haven't used it before, just to get the hang of how it comes out of the tube; it's very similar to icing a cake. Believe it or not, the cool blue metallic card used for the parcel was, in another life, and elegant Christmas cracker.

**You will need**

Blank pale blue card, 100 x 210mm (4 x 8¼in)

A4 sheet of multicoloured holographic paper

Blue metallic card, 45mm (1¾in) square

Scrap of blue or white card

Orange glitter glue

Tracing paper and pencil

Scissors and /or curved cuticle scissors

Steel ruler, craft knife and cutting mat

Double-sided tape and glue stick

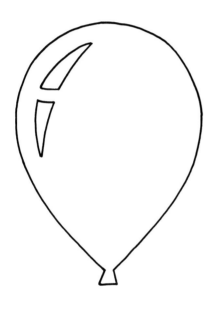

*Template, actual size*

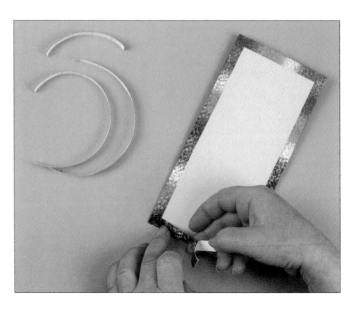

1. Cut four strips of holographic paper 10mm (½in) wide, two to fit the length of the card (stick these down first) then two for the top and bottom. If possible try to cut so that the corner colours match.

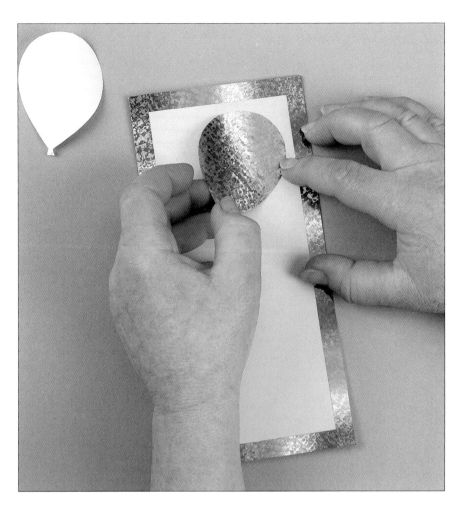

2. Transfer the balloon on to the back of the holographic paper, then cut it out. Stick the balloon at a slight angle towards the top right corner.

**Tip**
It is much easier to cut curves and circles with a pair of curved cuticle scissors.

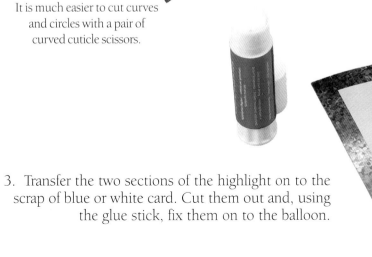

3. Transfer the two sections of the highlight on to the scrap of blue or white card. Cut them out and, using the glue stick, fix them on to the balloon.

4. Stick pieces of double-sided tape on to the back of the metallic card (parcel) and position it at a slight angle in the bottom left corner.

5. Using the glitter glue, draw a wavy line from the balloon to the top centre of the parcel; then draw a vertical and a horizontal line through the centre; and finally a bow at the top.

6. Leave the card flat for an hour or so, until the glitter glue has dried. Put a weight on the side to prevent the card from springing open.

*Opposite: This is a very simple design but made interesting by the fabulous multicoloured holographic paper and glitter glue.*

26

**Top:** *Utterly simple. Silver confetti balloons; lovely slightly mottled translucent paper (like thick tracing paper) and torn pieces of white mulberry tissue to give an impression of floating clouds.*

**Bottom:** *More metallic confetti balloons, coloured and very tiny, on a matt white card surrounded by metallic green. The strings (fine metallic gold thread) were sewn on to the white card and wound down the front and up the back, caught in a little V on the bottom edge.*

28

*Another version of the original card using scrunched cooking foil and dark
blue mulberry tissue as the background. The balloon was coated with PVA
glue and liberally sprinkled with glitter. The parcel was a chocolate wrapper
and the parcel string a glittery pipe cleaner.*

# Brilliant Butterflies

Stamped images of butterflies are so intricate that it would be impossible to replicate them in any other form. Using a lovely sparkly embossing powder on a strong background colour works well and very little else is needed, perhaps just some simple flower shapes.

Here I have printed the flowers on to shiny fluorescent card then cut them out. This particular card is too shiny to absorb the normal printing ink so I used embossing powder.

Be cautious when using the heat gun on these wonderful finished papers; they often contain plastic which will distort the image when excessive heat is applied. Always test the paper first.

## You will need

Blank turquoise card, 140mm (5½in) square

Shiny fluorescent card, 100mm (4in) square

White sparkle card, 25mm (1in) square

Butterfly and flower stamps

Embossing inkpad, embossing pen and heat gun

Green and sparkle-white embossing powders

Scissors and office hole punch

Double-sided tape and 3D foam squares

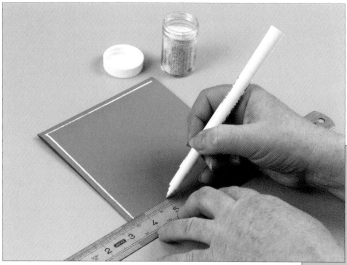

1. Using the embossing pen, draw one border line, sprinkle immediately with white glitter powder then apply the heat gun. Repeat with the other three lines.

2. Press the butterfly stamp on to the embossing pad, then press diagonally on to the card.

3. Sprinkle the image liberally with the sparkle-white powder.

4. Gently tap the side of the card to remove excess powder, then apply the heat gun.

**Tip**
If you can only find shiny fluorescent paper, perhaps gift wrap, simply stick it on to a piece of thin card using a glue stick.

5. Stamp the flowers on to the fluorescent card and, using the green embossing powder and heat gun, create six flower heads. Cut them out leaving a narrow border all the way round.

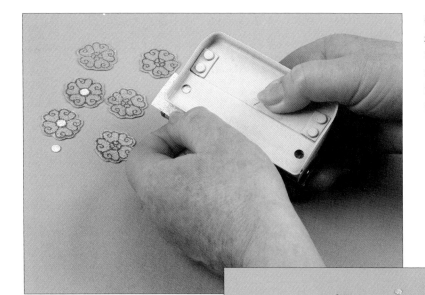

6. Stick a strip of double-sided tape on to the back of the white glitter card. Using the office hole punch, cut the flower centres then stick them on to the flowers.

7. Stick a strip of double-sided tape on to the back of the remaining fluorescent card. Using the office punch, cut nine discs then stick them on to three corners of the card.

8. Put a piece of double-sided tape on to the back of four flowers, and 3D foam squares on to two. Position them in the top left corner of the card.

*Sparkle-white embossing powder is really effective on a strongly coloured background.*
*This card is simple to produce and can be completed in very little time.*

**Left:** *This card is for someone special. It takes a little time to produce but the fact that the reverse image of the fluttering butterflies can be seen in the mirrored foil card makes all the effort worthwhile. And they really do flutter! The butterflies were stuck on to holographic paper, the same as the inlay, with sparkly thread running between them.*

**Above, left:** *I saw these little butterfly stickers at my local general store and thought how pretty they were. The floral paper is actually a thin printed tissue paper used as gift wrap. The tiny dots of gold were the remains of the outline sticker flowers used for the card on page 40.*

**Above, right:** *For this card, ordinary craft tissue paper was torn roughly into petal shapes, stuck down at the centre, then discs of glitter card and blobs of glitter glue were applied to create the flower centre. Watercolour paints were used in the butterfly wings to replicate the coloured petals.*

# Flashy Flowers

Like balloons, flowers are a perfect subject for glitter cards because of their general appeal and versatility; they can herald any number of different celebrations.

The exciting element here is the wonderfully changing colour of the pearlescent card. Just hold a piece and tip it slightly one way, then another, and see the orange turn into yellow and green, then bright pink. Amazing! The orange and green cards were originally two small carrier bags.

## You will need

Blank cream card, 140mm (5½in) square

Orange and green pearlescent cards, 120mm (4¾in) square

Green tinsel thread

Strip of gold glittered card, 25 x 50mm (1 x 2in)

Flower and office hole punches

Craft knife, scissors, circle cutter and cutting mat

Double-sided tape and 3D foam squares

Tracing paper, ruler and pencil

*Templates, actual size*

1. Mark the centre of the green square. Adjust the circle cutter to cut a 90mm (3½in) diameter circle. Position the point, and then make the cut.

2. Use double-sided tape to secure the square to the cream card, then transfer the large flower to the back of the circle.

3. Transfer the medium flower and the flower centre to the orange card, then cut out both flowers and the centre.

4. Punch sixteen flowers from the remaining orange card and put a small piece of double-sided tape on the back of each one.

5. Take your ruler diagonally across (corner to corner) and make marks for four flowers. Now find the centre of each side and mark where the top, bottom and two side flowers should be. It will be easy to position the remaining eight after the first eight have been stuck down.

6. Stick a strip of double-sided tape on the back of the gold glittered card. Using the office punch, cut seventeen circles. Stick one on to the orange flower centre and the remaining in the centre of each little flower.

**Tip**

Save a piece of backing from your double-sided tape. Cut a piece of tape to fit the backing. Put the two together. Use an office hole punch to make small circles. These can be used as neat adhesive for punched flowers and other small items.

7. Put four 3D foam squares on the underside of the orange flower and attach it to the green one. Cut four 40mm (1½in) lengths of tinsel thread and position them between the petals using thin strips of double-sided tape.

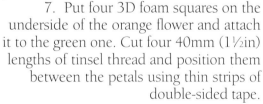

8. Use double-sided tape to secure the flower centre, and five 3D foam squares to stick the flower on to the card.

38

*Pearlescent, colour-changing card is the dominant element here. The
glittering gold flower centres were cut, using an office hole punch, from an
old Christmas card. 3D foam squares give depth to the central flower.*

**Left, top:** *Here is a gold theme, contrasting matt and shiny textured papers. The fine gold flowers are little outline stickers and the flowers in the bunch were cut using a craft punch. The stems are glitter glue and the blue, magical holographic card was cut from a Christmas carrier bag.*

**Left, bottom:** *The same flower shape as used in this project is used again in a single format for this card. Bronze and orange in contrasting matt and shine give an interesting effect. The flower centres are circles of tinsel thread stuck down with double-sided tape. The orange 'jewels' are blobs of glitter glue.*

**Right:** *I thought about little flowers hiding in the grass for this card. The colours are unreal, but that's OK. The card itself is a shiny royal blue. Tapering strips of pearlescent card were stuck down, with very fine strips of pink holographic paper stuck on some of them. The flowers were cut from the same paper, some hiding and some raised using 3D foam squares.*

# Fabulous Fairy Dust

This project brings to mind the character of Tinkerbell from *Peter Pan* and the trail of sparkly dust she left as she flew about performing mischief.

I have used stamps for these cards because they are so pretty, beautifully detailed and lend themselves to delicate sparkling effects. To achieve the best results for the semi-transparent look on the dress and wings, you will need to use watercolour paints, watercolour paper and a brush with a fine point. The technique is to lay a flat wash, then remove some of the colour using a clean, damp brush. In order to make a colour paler you simply add water; never add white paint. Have a little practice before starting. The open-weave tissue paper is very soft and easy to tear if you hold it firmly.

## You will need

Blank white card,
100 x 135mm (4 x 5¼in)

Blue sparkle card,
90 x 125mm (3½ x 5in)

White open-weave tissue,
90 x 125mm (3½ x 5in)

Watercolour paints

Watercolour paper,
90 x 125mm (3½ x 5in)

Paintbrush with a fine point

Fairy stamp

Sparkle-silver and sparkle-white embossing powders

Embossing inkpad and embossing heat gun

Tracing paper and pencil

Scissors and/or cuticle scissors

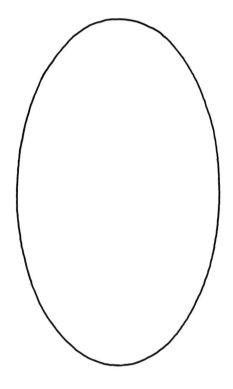

*Template, actual size*

1. Put pieces of double-sided tape on to the back of the blue sparkle card and position it centrally on to the blank white card.

**Tip**

When using the heat gun, watch carefully for the powder to melt, just a few seconds, then remove the heat gun immediately to avoid scorching the paper.

2. Press the stamp on to the embossing inkpad. Stamp it on to the centre of the watercolour paper. Sprinkle the image liberally with the silver powder.

3. Have ready a sheet of spare paper, then tap the watercolour paper on its side to remove the excess powder. Pour the powder back into its container. Use the heat gun to melt the powder.

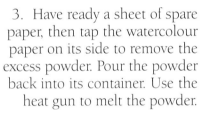

4. Paint the fairy, removing some areas of colour with a clean, damp brush to give a semi-transparent effect. I used French ultramarine for the dress, cerulean blue for the wings and very watery alizarin crimson with a touch of cadmium yellow for the skin tone.

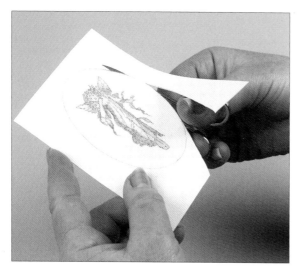

5. Transfer the oval to the watercolour paper, then carefully cut it out, using a pair of cuticle scissors if you have some.

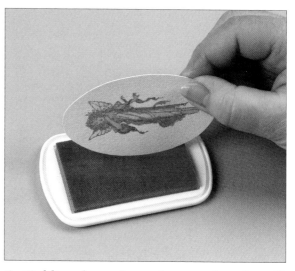

6. Holding the oval, gently press the edge, all the way round, on to the embossing pad. Sprinkle liberally with the white powder then use the heat gun to melt it, just as before.

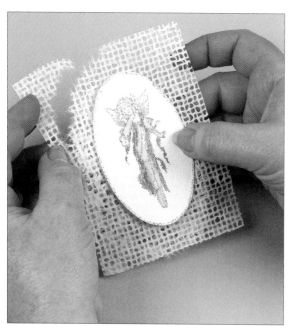

7. Put a piece of double-sided tape on to the back of the oval, then attach it to the centre of the open-weave tissue paper. Carefully tear the tissue following the curve of the oval.

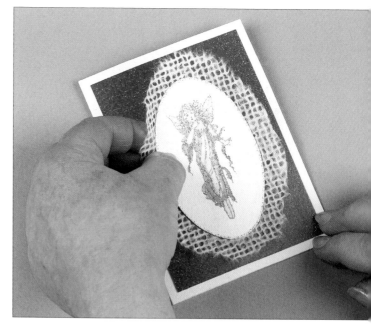

8. Attach the oval and tissue paper to the card using double-sided tape.

*An oval seemed to be the perfect shape to frame this little fairy, backed by an open-weave tissue paper to soften the shape.*

*This fairy stamp is quite complex – the added lavender, leaves and butterfly mean that the design of the card should be very simple. When painting the fairy I tried to replicate the soft rainbow colours of the foil paper (originally gift wrap). Notice how some of the paint has been removed from the dress and wings to give a feeling of lightness.*

**Top:** *This reminds me of those charming Parisian net hats of the fifties, simple and alluring. A square of purple card was covered with glitter net. Another length was gathered, tied with silver thread and attached to the card with double-sided tape. The oval was positioned and the sides of the net tucked into the sides of the square.*

**Bottom:** *It is very difficult to emboss successfully on mulberry tissue. Here I have used ordinary tissue, in the same delicate pink, and stuck it on top of the torn mulberry tissue using just a sliver of double-sided tape. It is even possible to paint on the ordinary tissue without causing it to cockle. The little glittery flowers were punched from an old birthday card.*

# Index